TEMP

Teatime
TREATS

Your Promise of Success

Welcome to the world of Confident Cooking, created for you in
our test kitchen, where recipes are double-tested by our team
of home economists to achieve a high standard of success.

MURDOCH BOOKS®
Sydney • London • Vancouver

Traditional Favourites

What could be more reassuring and relaxing than a leisurely afternoon tea? Get out your best cups and saucers, set a pretty table and take the time to make some of these classic recipes, to remind your guests of the peaceful days of old.

Chelsea Buns

Preparation time:
  20 minutes +1 hour
  20 minutes standing
Total cooking time:
  20 minutes
Makes 24

7 g sachet dried yeast
1 teaspoon sugar
1 tablespoon plain flour
1/2 cup milk, warmed
21/2 cups plain flour,
  sifted
125 g butter, chopped
1 tablespoon sugar
1/2 teaspoon mixed spice
1 egg, lightly beaten
2 teaspoons grated
  lemon rind
60 g butter, extra
1/4 cup soft brown sugar
1 cup mixed dried fruit
1/2 teaspoon mixed
  spice, extra

Glaze
1 tablespoon milk
2 tablespoons sugar

1. Line 30 x 25 x 2 cm shallow Swiss roll tin with baking paper. Combine yeast, sugar and flour in a small mixing bowl. Gradually add milk; blend until smooth. Stand, covered with plastic wrap, in warm place 10 minutes or until foamy.
2. Place flour, butter, sugar and spice in food processor bowl. Using the pulse action, press button for 30 seconds or until mixture is fine and crumbly. Add egg, rind and yeast mixture process for15 seconds or until mixture almost forms a dough.
3. Turn mixture onto lightly floured surface, knead for about 2 minutes or until dough is smooth; shape into a ball. Place in large, lightly oiled mixing bowl. Leave, covered with plastic wrap, in warm place for

Chelsea Buns (left)
and Chocolate Gateau (page 4).

1 hour or until well risen. Knead dough again 2 minutes or until smooth.

4. Preheat oven to moderately hot 210°C (gas 190°C). Using electric beaters, beat extra butter and the sugar in small mixing bowl until light and creamy. Roll dough out to 40 x 35 cm rectangle. Spread butter and sugar all over the dough to within 2 cm of edge of one of the longer sides. Spread with combined fruit and extra spice.

5. Roll dough lengthways, firmly and evenly into a log, Swiss roll style, to enclose fruit and butter mixture. Using a sharp knife, cut roll into 24 slices. Arrange slices evenly apart on prepared tray. Leave, covered with plastic wrap, in warm place for 10 minutes or until well risen.

6. Bake buns for 20 minutes or until well browned and cooked through. Remove from oven; brush liberally with glaze. Transfer to wire rack to cool.

7. *To make Glaze:* Combine milk and sugar in pan. Stir over low heat until sugar dissolves and mixture is almost boiling. Remove from heat.

Chocolate Gateau

Preparation time:
 40 minutes
Total cooking time:
 30 minutes
Makes 23 cm cake

2 cups sugar
2 cups water
250 g unsalted butter
1/2 cup cocoa powder
1 teaspoon bicarbonate
 of soda
3 cups self-raising
 flour
4 eggs, lightly beaten

Mock Cream
1/2 cup caster sugar
1/2 cup water
250 g unsalted butter

Chocolate Icing
90 g dark chocolate,
 chopped
15 g butter
60 g white chocolate,
 chopped

1. Preheat oven to a moderate 180°C. Brush two 23 cm shallow round cake tins with melted butter or oil. Line base and sides with paper; grease paper.

2. Combine sugar, water, butter, cocoa and soda in large pan. Stir over low heat until mixture comes to the boil, reduce heat and

simmer for 3 minutes. Transfer mixture to large mixing bowl, cool to lukewarm.

3. Stir in sifted flour and eggs. Beat with wooden spoon until just combined; do not overbeat. Pour mixture into prepared tins; smooth surface. Bake 30 minutes or until skewer comes out clean when inserted into centre of cake. Stand cake in tin 3 minutes before turning onto wire rack to cool.

4. *To make Mock Cream:* Combine sugar and water in small pan. Stir constantly over low heat until sugar has dissolved and mixture boils. Remove from heat; cool. Beat butter in small mixing bowl until light and creamy. Pour cooled syrup in a thin stream over creamed butter, beating constantly for 3–4 minutes or until mixture is glossy and smooth.

5. *To make Chocolate Icing:* Combine dark chocolate and butter in a pan. Stir constantly over low heat until chocolate melts; remove from heat. Spread chocolate evenly over top layer of cake. Melt white chocolate in same way as dark chocolate. Place into small paper piping bag, seal open end. Snip tip off piping

Streusel Teacake.

bag; drizzle chocolate decoratively over cake.

6. *To assemble cake:* Place plain cake layer on a serving plate. Spread cake evenly with half of the mock cream. Pipe an edge around rim of cake with remaining mock cream. Place iced layer on top.

Note: Decorated cake can be made day before required. Do not refrigerate. Cover and store in cool place.

Streusel Teacake

Preparation time:
  30 minutes
Total cooking time:
  25 minutes
Makes 17 cm round cake

1 egg
¹/2 cup sugar
¹/2 cup milk
1 cup self-raising flour
125 g unsalted butter,
  melted

Streusel Layer
¹/2 cup plain flour
60 g unsalted butter
¹/4 cup soft brown sugar

Topping
30 g unsalted butter,
  melted
1 teaspoon ground
  cinnamon
1 tablespoon sugar

1. Preheat oven to moderate 180°C. Brush a deep round 17 cm cake tin with melted butter or oil.

2. Using electric beaters, beat egg in small mixing bowl for 5 minutes or until thick and pale. Add sugar gradually, beating constantly until dissolved and mixture is pale yellow and glossy.

3. Stir in milk. Using a metal spoon, fold in sifted flour and melted butter quickly and lightly.

4. *To make Streusel Layer:* Sift flour into medium bowl, add chopped butter and sugar. Using fingertips, rub butter into flour for 2 minutes or until the mixture is fine and crumbly.

5. Spread half cake mixture into prepared tin; sprinkle over streusel layer and spread remaining cake mixture over. Bake for 25 minutes or until skewer comes out clean when inserted into centre of cake. Stand cake in tin 5 minutes before turning out on wire rack to cool.

For Topping: Brush cake with melted butter and sprinkle with combined cinnamon and sugar.

Cranberry Muffins

Preparation time:
  20 minutes
Total cooking time:
  20 minutes
Makes 12

2¹/2 cups self-raising
  flour
²/3 cup caster sugar
¹/4 cup chopped pecan
  nuts
1 teaspoon finely grated
  lemon rind
1 egg, lightly beaten
1 cup milk
90 g butter, melted
¹/2 cup whole cranberry
  sauce

1. Preheat oven to moderately hot 210°C (gas 190°C). Brush melted butter or oil into 12 muffin cups (¹/3-cup capacity). Sift flour into a large mixing bowl. Add sugar, pecans and lemon rind, stir until combined. Make a well in the centre.

2. Combine egg, milk and butter in a small mixing bowl, add all at once to dry ingredients. Using a wooden spoon, stir until ingredients are just combined; do not overbeat.

3. Spoon half the mixture into prepared muffin cups. Top each muffin with cranberry sauce. Spoon remaining mixture over cranberry sauce.

4. Bake 20 minutes or until puffed and golden brown. Turn onto wire rack to cool.

Caramel Hazelnut Scrolls

Preparation time:
  20 minutes
Total cooking time:
  25 minutes
Makes 16

2¹/2 cups self-raising
  flour
¹/2 cup caster sugar
125 g butter
¹/2 cup milk
¹/4 cup sour cream
60 g butter, extra,
  softened
¹/3 cup soft brown sugar,
  firmly packed
¹/3 cup chopped
  hazelnuts

Caramel Icing
45 g butter
¹/4 cup soft brown
  sugar, firmly packed
1 tablespoon milk
¹/2 cup icing sugar,
  sifted

1. Preheat oven to moderately hot 210°C (gas 190°C). Brush a shallow 23 cm square cake tin with melted butter. Sift flour into a large mixing bowl; add sugar and butter. Using fingertips, rub butter into flour for 2 minutes or until the mixture is fine and crumbly.

Cranberry Muffins (top) and Caramel Hazelnut Scrolls.

Add combined milk and sour cream to bowl, stir until ingredients are just combined and the mixture almost smooth.
2. Turn dough onto lightly floured surface. Knead for 1 minute or until smooth. Roll out dough on lightly floured surface to a 40 x 30 cm rectangle. Combine extra butter, brown sugar and hazelnuts in mixing bowl. Crumble mixture evenly over dough.
3. Roll dough from the long side into a log, Swiss roll style. Using a sharp knife, cut into 16 even slices. Place slices in prepared tin. Bake for 25 minutes or until cakes sound hollow when tapped. Turn onto a wire rack, turn right side up.
4. *To make Caramel Icing:* Melt butter in a small saucepan, add brown sugar and milk. Stir over low heat for 1 minute or until bubbly. Add sifted icing sugar, stir over low heat for 1 minute or until mixture is smooth. Spread cake with caramel icing while icing and cake are still hot, allow to cool. Sprinkle with extra chopped hazelnuts, if desired.

Stand yeast mixture in warm place for
10 minutes or until foamy.

Add milk, egg, butter and yeast to flour
and mix to dough with a knife.

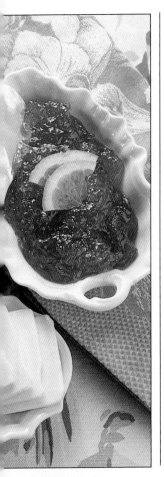

English Muffins

Preparation time:
  20 minutes + 1 hour
  40 minutes standing
Total cooking time:
  16 minutes
Makes 15

7 g sachet dried yeast
1/2 teaspoon sugar
1 teaspoon plain flour
1/4 cup warm water
4 cups plain flour, extra
1 teaspoon salt
1 1/3 cups lukewarm milk
1 egg, lightly beaten
40 g butter, melted

1. Lightly dust two 32 x 28 cm oven trays with flour. Combine yeast, sugar, flour and water in small bowl; blend until smooth. Stand, covered with plastic wrap, in a warm place 10 minutes or until foamy. Sift extra flour and salt into large bowl.

2. Make a well in centre, add milk, egg, butter and yeast mixture. Using a knife, mix to a soft dough.

3. Turn dough onto lightly floured surface, knead for 2 minutes or until smooth. Shape dough into ball, place in large, lightly oiled bowl. Leave, covered with plastic wrap, in warm place 1 1/2 hours or until well risen.

4. Preheat oven to moderately hot 210°C (gas 190°C).Knead dough again for 2 minutes or until smooth. Roll dough to 1 cm thickness. Cut into rounds with an 8 cm cutter. Place rounds onto prepared oven trays. Leave, covered with plastic wrap, in warm place 10 minutes.

5. Bake muffins for 8 minutes, turn over and bake 8 minutes more.

English Muffins.

Knead dough for 2 minutes or until smooth, shape into a ball.

Roll dough to 1 cm thickness, cut into rounds with an 8 cm cutter.

9

Sour Cream Pound Cake

Preparation time:
  10 minutes
Total cooking time:
  30 minutes
*Makes 20 cm round
cake*

100 g unsalted butter
2/3 cup caster sugar
2 eggs, lightly beaten
1/2 teaspoon vanilla
  essence
1 1/4 cups self-raising
  flour, sifted
1/2 cup sour cream

1. Preheat oven to
moderate 180°C. Brush
a deep 20 cm cake tin
with oil, line base with
paper; grease paper.
2. Using electric
beaters, beat butter and
sugar in mixing bowl
until light and creamy.
Add eggs gradually,
beating well after each
addition. Add essence;
beat until combined.
3. Transfer mixture to
large mixing bowl.
Using a metal spoon,
fold in flour and cream.
Stir until just combined
and mixture is smooth.
4. Spoon mixture into
prepared tin; smooth
surface. Bake for
30 minutes or until
skewer comes out clean
when inserted in centre
of cake. Turn onto wire
rack to cool. Dust cake
with icing sugar.

Devonshire Splits (Cream Buns)

Preparation time:
  30 minutes + 1 hour
  15 minutes standing
Total cooking time:
  20 minutes
Makes 12

3 1/2 cups plain flour,
  sifted
2 tablespoons sugar
pinch salt
1 1/3 cups milk, warmed
60 g butter, melted
7 g sachet dried yeast
1 1/4 cups cream
1 tablespoon icing sugar
1/2 cup raspberry jam
2 tablespoons icing
  sugar, extra

1. Line base of a 32 x
28 cm oven tray with
paper; grease paper.
Dust tin lightly with
flour; shake off excess.
2. Place flour, sugar
and salt in food
processor bowl.
Combine milk and
butter in a small bowl.
Sprinkle yeast into milk
mixture, stir to dissolve.
Pour yeast mixture onto
dry ingredients.
3. Using the pulse
action, press button for
30 seconds or until a
soft, smooth dough
forms. Transfer dough
to a lightly oiled mixing
bowl. Leave, covered

with plastic wrap, in
warm place for 1 hour
or until well risen.
4. Turn dough onto
lightly floured surface,
knead for about
2 minutes or until
smooth. Divide dough
into 12 pieces. Knead
one portion at a time
on lightly floured
surface for 30 seconds,
shape into a ball.
Repeat process with
remaining dough.
5. Preheat oven to
moderately hot 210°C
(190°C gas). Place balls
of dough evenly apart
on prepared tray.
Leave, covered with
plastic wrap, in warm
place for 15 minutes or
until well risen. Bake
20 minutes or until well
browned and cooked
through. Stand for
5 minutes before
transferring to wire
rack to cool.
6. Using a serrated
knife, cut diagonally
into the bun, to a depth
of 10 cm from top of
bun towards the base.
Using electric beaters,
beat cream and sugar in
small mixing bowl until
firm peaks form.
Fill the buns with the
whipped cream and
jam. Dust with icing
sugar before serving.

Note: Best filled close
to serving time.

*Devonshire Splits (top) and
Sour Cream Pound Cake.*

Mini Lemon Pikelets

Preparation time:
  10 minutes
Total cooking time:
  4 minutes per batch
Makes about 25

1 cup self-raising flour
1/3 cup caster sugar
2 teaspoons finely
  grated lemon rind
1 egg, lightly beaten
1/2 cup milk
1/3 cup lemon butter
3/4 cup cream,
  whipped

1. Sift flour into a medium mixing bowl, add sugar and lemon rind, stir until combined; make a well in the centre.
2. Combine egg and milk in a small bowl, add to flour mixture all at once. Using a wooden spoon, stir until all the liquid is incorporated and batter is free of lumps.
3. Brush base of a frying pan lightly with melted butter. Drop heaped teaspoonsful of mixture onto base of pan about 3 cm apart. Cook over medium heat 2 minutes or until underside is golden. Turn pikelets over and cook other side.
4. Remove from pan; repeat process with remaining mixture.

Serve topped with lemon butter and whipped cream.

Note: If the pan is too hot or over-greased, surface of pikelets will be uneven.

Cherry Ripple Teacake

Preparation time:
  30 minutes
Total cooking time:
  35–40 minutes
Makes 20 cm ring cake

750 g jar pitted cherries
1 tablespoon cornflour
1/2 cup reserved cherry
  syrup
2 cups self-raising
  flour
3/4 cup sugar
1/3 cup desiccated
  coconut
125 g butter, chopped
1 egg
3/4 cup milk

1. Preheat oven to moderate 180°C. Brush a 20 cm ring tin with melted butter or oil. Line base and sides with paper; grease paper.

2. Place drained cherries into medium pan, blend cornflour with reserved syrup, add to cherries. Stir over low heat until mixture boils and thickens. Set aside to cool.
3. Sift flour into large mixing bowl; add sugar, coconut and butter. Using fingertips, rub butter into flour mixture for 2–3 minutes or until mixture is fine and crumbly. Measure out half cup of mixture and reserve for top.
4. Add combined egg and milk to bowl and stir until mixture is almost smooth. Spoon two-thirds of mixture into prepared tin; smooth surface. Carefully spoon on cooled cherry mixture. Spoon remaining mixture in small mounds on top of surface, sprinkle over reserved half cup flour mixture.
5. Bake for 35–40 minutes or until a skewer comes out clean when inserted into centre of cake. Stand cake in tin 10 minutes before turning onto wire rack to cool.

Note: Any canned berries can be used.

Cherry Ripple Teacake (top) and Mini Lemon Pikelets.

Chocolate Raspberry Swiss Roll

Preparation time:
  25 minutes
Total cooking time:
  12–15 minutes
Makes one Swiss roll

½ cup self-raising flour
¼ cup cocoa powder
3 eggs
½ cup caster sugar
¼ cup grated dark
    chocolate
1 tablespoon hot water
1 tablespoon caster
    sugar, extra
1¼ cups cream, softly
    whipped
1 packet frozen raspberries

1. Preheat oven to moderate 180°C. Brush a 30 x 25 x 2 cm Swiss roll tin with oil. Line base and two sides with paper; grease paper. Sift flour and cocoa three times onto greaseproof paper.
2. Using electric beaters, beat eggs in bowl for 4–5 minutes or until thick and pale. Add sugar gradually, beating constantly until mixture is pale, yellow and glossy. Transfer mixture to large bowl.
3. Using a metal spoon, fold in sifted flour, cocoa, chocolate and water quickly and lightly. Spread mixture evenly into tin; smooth surface. Bake 12–15 minutes, until lightly golden and springy.
4. Place sheet of greaseproof paper on a dry tea-towel. Sprinkle with extra sugar. Turn cake onto paper; stand 2 minutes. Carefully roll cake up with paper; stand 5 minutes. Unroll cake, discard paper. Spread with whipped cream and raspberries; reroll. Trim ends of roll.

Chocolate Raspberry Swiss Roll.

Brush Swiss roll tin with oil, line base and sides with paper, grease paper.

Using electric beaters, beat eggs, then add sugar gradually.

Fold in sifted flour, cocoa, chocolate and water with a metal spoon.

On dry tea-towel, sprinkle paper with sugar and roll up cake.

Orange Fig Cake

Preparation time:
  15 minutes
Total cooking time:
  1 hour 10 minutes
*Makes 20 cm round
cake*

125 g butter
1/2 cup soft brown
  sugar
1/2 cup honey
3 eggs, lightly beaten
1/2 cup chopped dried
  figs
2 teaspoons finely
  grated orange rind
1 small orange, peeled,
  chopped
1/2 cup oatbran
1 cup self-raising flour
1/4 cup milk

1. Preheat oven to
moderately slow 160°C.
Brush a deep, 20 cm
round cake tin with
melted butter or oil,
line base with paper;
grease paper. Using
electric beaters, beat
butter, sugar and honey
in small bowl until light
and creamy. Add eggs
gradually, beating after
each addition.
2. Transfer mixture to
large bowl; add figs,
orange rind and orange,
oatbran, sifted flour
and milk. Using a metal
spoon, stir until mixture
is combined.

3. Pour mixture into
prepared tin; smooth
surface. Bake for
1 hour 10 minutes or
until a skewer comes
out clean when inserted
in centre of cake. Leave
cake in tin 5 minutes
before turning onto
wire rack to cool. Dust
with icing sugar.

Hazelnut and Coffee Cream Gateau

Preparation time:
  30 minutes
Total cooking time:
  20 minutes
*Makes 20 cm round
double layer cake*

2/3 cup self-raising
  flour
1/3 cup cornflour
4 eggs
2/3 cup caster sugar
1 tablespoon instant
  coffee powder
1 tablespoon hot water
1/4 cup ground
  hazelnuts
1/4 teaspoon ground
  cinnamon, for dusting

Filling
1 cup cream
1/4 cup icing sugar
1 teaspoon instant
  coffee powder, extra
1 teaspoon hot water,
  extra

1. Preheat oven to
moderate 180°C. Brush
two shallow 20 cm
round cake tins with
melted butter or oil.
Line base with paper;
grease paper. Dust tins
lightly with flour, shake
off excess. Sift flour
and cornflour three
times onto greaseproof
paper.
2. Using electric
beaters, beat eggs in
small mixing bowl for
2 minutes or until thick
and pale. Add sugar
gradually, beating
constantly until
dissolved and mixture
is pale yellow and
glossy. Transfer mixture
to large mixing bowl.
3. Using a metal spoon,
fold in combined coffee
and water, hazelnuts
and flours quickly and
lightly.
4. Spread mixture
evenly in prepared tins.
Bake for 20 minutes or
until sponges are lightly
golden and shrink from
side of the tins. Turn
onto wire rack to cool.
5. *To make Filling:*
Using electric beaters,
beat cream, icing sugar
and combined extra
coffee and water in
small mixing bowl until
soft peaks form.
6. Place first cake layer
on a board. Spread
evenly with filling. Place
remaining cake on top.
Transfer to serving
plate. Dust top of cake
with cinnamon.

---

*Hazelnut and Coffee Cream Gateau (top)
and Orange Fig Cake.*

Cherry, Date and Walnut Roll

Preparation time:
  15 minutes
Total cooking time:
  50 minutes + 15
  minutes standing
Makes one nut roll

1/2 cup (70 g) finely
  chopped fresh dates
2 tablespoons currants
1/3 cup water
1/3 cup soft brown sugar
40 g butter
1/2 teaspoon
  bicarbonate of soda
1/2 cup chopped
  walnuts
1/4 cup chopped glacé
  cherries
1/2 teaspoon ground
  nutmeg
1 egg, lightly beaten
3/4 cup self-raising flour,
  sifted

1. Preheat oven to
moderate 180°C. Brush
a nut roll tin (4-cup
capacity) with melted
butter or oil. Line side
with paper; grease
paper.
2. Place dates, currants,
water, sugar and butter
in small pan. Stir over
low heat 5 minutes or
until butter has melted
and mixture boils.
Remove pan from heat,
cool slightly. Add soda
to pan; stir.

3. Place walnuts,
cherries, nutmeg, egg,
cooled date mixture
and flour into large
mixing bowl. Stir with
a wooden spoon until
just combined.
4. Spoon mixture into
prepared tin; close open
end of tin with lid. Lay
tin on its side in oven,
bake 45 minutes. Leave
cake in tin 15 minutes
before transferring to
wire rack to cool.

> **HINT**
> Serve roll cut into
> slices spread with
> cream cheese or your
> favourite fruit butter.

Lemon and Pecan Syrup Loaf

Preparation time:
  15 minutes
Total cooking time:
  45 minutes
*Makes 25 x 15 x 5.5 cm
loaf*

1 1/4 cups self-raising
  flour
125 g unsalted butter,
  chopped
3/4 cup caster sugar
2 eggs
1/3 cup milk
1/2 cup coarsely
  chopped pecan nuts
1 tablespoon grated
  lemon rind

Lemon Syrup
1/4 cup lemon juice
2 tablespoons water
1/2 cup caster sugar
50 g butter

1. Preheat oven to
moderate 180°C. Brush
25 x 15 x 5.5 cm loaf
tin with melted butter
or oil. Cover base with
paper, extending over

*Lemon and Pecan Syrup Loaf (left)
and Cherry, Date and Walnut Roll.*

two sides; grease paper.
2. Place flour in food processor bowl; add butter and sugar. Using the pulse action, press button for 20 seconds or until mixture is fine and crumbly.
3. Add combined eggs and milk to bowl, process 10 seconds or until just combined.

Add nuts and rind, process 5 seconds. Spoon mixture into prepared tin; smooth surface. Bake for 45 minutes or until skewer comes out clean when inserted in centre of cake. Leave cake in the tin.
4. *To make Lemon Syrup:* Place juice,

water, sugar and butter in a small pan. Stir over medium heat for 2 minutes or until sugar has dissolved and mixture boils. Reduce heat, simmer, uncovered, 3 minutes. Pour cooled lemon syrup over the hot cake or hot syrup over cooled cake in tin.

Buttermilk Scones

Preparation time:
 15 minutes
Total cooking time:
 10–12 minutes
Makes 12

2 cups self-raising flour
1 tablespoon sugar
60 g butter
³/4 cup buttermilk or
 ¹/2 cup milk and
 ¹/4 cup sour cream
jam and whipped cream
 to serve

1. Preheat oven to
moderate 180°C. Dust
a 30 x 28 cm oven tray
lightly with flour.
2. Sift flour and sugar
into large mixing bowl;
add chopped butter.
3. Using fingertips, rub
butter into flour for
1 minute or until mixture
is fine and crumbly. Add
buttermilk, stir until a
soft dough is formed.
4. Turn out onto lightly
floured surface and
knead lightly until
dough is no longer
sticky. Press dough to
1 cm in thickness. Cut
into rounds, with plain
or fluted 5 cm cutter.
5. Place rounds just
touching on prepared
tray. Bake for
10–12 minutes or until
golden brown.
6. Serve scones warm
with apricot or
strawberry jam and
softly whipped cream.

Crumpets

Preparation time:
 25 minutes +
 1 hour 25 minutes
Total cooking time:
 6 minutes
Makes 12–14

7 g sachet dried yeast
1 teaspoon sugar
1³/4 cups warm water
3 cups plain flour
2 tablespoons
 powdered milk
1 teaspoon bicarbonate
 soda
2 tablespoons warm
 water
30 g butter, melted

1. Combine yeast, sugar
and water in medium
mixing bowl. Stand,
covered with plastic
wrap, in warm place for
about 10 minutes or
until foamy.
2. Sift flour and
powdered milk into
large mixing bowl.
Make a well in the
centre, add yeast
mixture. Using a
wooden spoon, mix to
a soft dough. Stand
covered in a warm
place for 1 hour or
until well risen and
surface is bubbly.
3. Add combined soda
and warm water, stir
well. Stand mixture for
15 minutes.
4. Lightly brush a large
frying pan with melted
butter. Place greased

egg rings in pan. Place
enough mixture in each
ring to come to top of
ring. Cook over
medium heat for 4–5
minutes or until
bubbles appear on top.
5. Remove ring, turn
crumpet over, cook
30 seconds. Remove
from pan. Toast
crumpets, serve.

Easy Sponge with Jam and Cream

Preparation time:
 15 minutes
Total cooking time:
 20 minutes +
 5 minutes standing
*Makes 20 cm round
double layer cake*

¹/2 cup plain flour
¹/4 cup cornflour
3 eggs
¹/3 cup caster sugar
30 g butter, melted
¹/2 teaspoon vanilla
 essence
2 tablespoons raspberry
 jam
²/3 cup cream
1 tablespoon icing sugar
2 tablespoons icing
 sugar, extra

1. Preheat oven to
moderate 180°C. Brush
two shallow 20 cm
round cake tins with oil.
Line base with paper;
grease paper. Dust tins
lightly with flour; shake
off excess.
2. Sift flour and

Clockwise from left: Buttermilk Scones, Easy Sponge with Jam and Cream, Crumpets.

cornflour three times onto greaseproof paper. Place eggs in a small mixing bowl. Using electric beaters, beat eggs on high speed for 2 minutes. Add sugar gradually, beating constantly 8 minutes or until dissolved and the mixture is pale yellow and glossy.

3. Transfer mixture to large mixing bowl. Using a metal spoon, fold in butter, essence and flours quickly and lightly. Spread mixture evenly into prepared tins. Bake 20 minutes or until sponges are lightly golden and shrink from side of tin. Remove from oven. Leave in tins

for 5 minutes before turning onto wire rack.

4. Spread jam over one sponge layer. Using electric beaters beat cream and icing sugar until firm peaks form. Spread or pipe cream over jam. Top with remaining sponge layer. Dust sponge with extra icing sugar.

21

Orange Bun

Preparation time:
  45 minutes + 1 hour
  5 minutes standing
Total cooking time:
  20 minutes
*Makes 23 cm round
with eight wedges*

2 cups plain flour
7 g sachet dried yeast
1/3 cup mixed peel
2 tablespoons caster
  sugar
2 teaspoons grated
  orange rind
1/3 cup warm milk
1/3 cup orange juice
1 egg, lightly beaten
30 g butter, melted

Glaze
1 tablespoon water
1 teaspoon sugar
1 teaspoon gelatine

1. Brush a deep 23 cm
round cake tin with
melted butter or oil. Sift
flour into a large mixing
bowl. Add yeast, mixed
peel, sugar and orange
rind, stir until combined.
Make a well in the centre.
2. Combine milk,
orange juice, egg and
butter in a small mixing
bowl, add to flour
mixture. Using a knife,
mix to a soft dough.
Turn onto lightly
floured surface, knead
for 10 minutes or until
dough is smooth and

elastic. To test, press a
finger into the dough.
When ready, the dough
will spring back
immediately and not
leave an indent.
3. Place dough into a
large, lightly oiled
mixing bowl. Leave,
covered with plastic
wrap, in warm place
for 45 minutes or until
well risen.
4. Knead dough again
for 1 minute or until
smooth. Press dough
into prepared cake tin.
Leave, covered with
plastic wrap, in warm
place for 20 minutes or
until well risen.
5. Preheat oven to
moderate 180°C. Cut
dough into eight wedges
by carefully making
deep cuts with a sharp
pointed, oiled knife. Be
careful not to push out
all the air. If the dough
deflates, simply stand
for another 5 minutes
or until risen.
6. Bake for 20 minutes
or until golden brown
and cooked through.
Dough should sound
hollow when tapped.
Turn onto wire rack.
7. *To make Glaze:*
Combine water, sugar
and gelatine in a small
mixing bowl. Place over
a pan of simmering
water, heat until sugar
and gelatine are
dissolved. Brush over
bun while still hot.

Lemon Banana Cake

Preparation time:
  20 minutes
Total cooking time:
  45 minutes
Makes 20 cm ring cake

11/2 cups self-raising flour
90 g butter, softened
1/2 cup caster sugar
1/2 cup desiccated
  coconut
2 teaspoons grated
  lemon rind

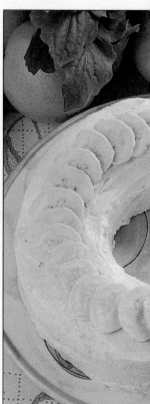

Lemon Banana Cake (left) and Orange Bun.

⅓ cup lemon juice
2 eggs, lightly beaten
¾ cup mashed, ripe
  banana

Cream Cheese Icing
90 g cream cheese
45 g butter
⅓ cup icing sugar
1 teaspoon grated
  lemon rind

1. Preheat oven to moderate 180°C. Brush a 20 cm ring tin with oil, dust lightly with flour, shake off excess.
2. Sift flour into a large mixing bowl. Add butter, sugar, coconut, lemon rind and juice, eggs and banana.
3. Using electric beaters, beat on low speed for 1 minute or until ingredients are just moistened. Beat on high speed for 2 minutes or until well combined and increased in volume.
4. Pour mixture evenly into prepared tin; smooth surface. Bake for 45 minutes or until lightly golden and a skewer comes out clean when inserted in cake.
5. Leave cake in tin for 3 minutes before turning onto wire rack to cool.
6. *To make Cream Cheese Icing:* Beat cream cheese and butter in small mixing bowl until light and creamy. Add icing sugar and lemon rind, beating for 2 minutes or until the mixture is smooth and fluffy.
7. Spread icing onto cooled cake.

Treacle and Malt Loaf

Preparation time:
  15 minutes +1 hour
  50 minutes standing
Total cooking time:
  40 minutes
Makes 1 loaf

1 cup lukewarm water
7 g sachet dried yeast
1 teaspoon sugar
2 cups plain wholemeal
  flour
1 cup plain flour
2 teaspoons ground
  cinnamon
1/2 cup raisins
30 g butter, melted
1 tablespoon treacle
1 tablespoon liquid
  malt extract
1 tablespoon hot milk
1/2 teaspoon malt, extra

1. Brush 21 x 14 x 7 cm loaf tin with oil.
2. Combine water, yeast and sugar in small bowl. Stand in warm position for 10 minutes or until foamy.
3. Sift flours and cinnamon into large mixing bowl, add raisins, stir to combine. Make a well in centre. Add melted butter, treacle, malt and yeast mixture. Using a knife, mix to a soft dough.
4. Turn dough onto lightly floured surface. Knead for 4 minutes or until smooth. Shape dough into ball, place

into lightly oiled mixing bowl. Stand, covered with plastic wrap, in warm place for 1 hour or until well risen.
5. Punch dough with fist. Knead again for 3 minutes or until smooth.
6. Arrange dough into tin. Stand, covered with plastic, in warm place 40 minutes or until well risen. Brush with combined milk and malt. Heat oven to moderate 180°C. Bake 40 minutes or until well browned and cooked through. Stand for 3 minutes in tin before transferring to wire rack to cool.

Note: This loaf is best eaten on day of baking. However, it can be frozen for a month.

Sacher Slice

Preparation time:
  15 minutes
Total cooking time:
  40 minutes + 30
  minutes refrigeration
Makes 30 x 20 cm slice

150 g dark chocolate,
  finely chopped
2 tablespoons
  chocolate-flavoured
  liqueur
125 g butter
1/2 cup sugar
4 eggs, separated
1/2 cup self-raising flour
1/2 cup plain flour

Icing
180 g dark chocolate,
  finely chopped
125 g butter
1 teaspoon chocolate-
  flavoured liqueur,
  extra

1. Preheat oven to moderate 180°C. Brush a shallow rectangular 30 x 20 cm cake tin with melted butter or oil. Line base and two sides with greaseproof paper, grease paper.
2. Place chocolate in small bowl. Stand bowl over simmering water and stir until chocolate is melted and smooth. Cool slightly, stir in liqueur.
3. Using electric beaters, beat butter and sugar in small mixing bowl until light and creamy. Add egg yolks gradually, beating thoroughly after each addition. Transfer mixture to large mixing bowl, stir in chocolate. Using metal spoon, fold in sifted flours.
4. Place egg whites in small, clean, dry mixing bowl. Using electric beaters, beat until soft peaks form. Using large metal spoon, fold egg whites into cake mixture.
5. Spoon mixture into prepared tin. Bake for 35 minutes or until a skewer comes out clean when inserted into the centre of slice. Stand in

Treacle and Malt Loaf (left) and Sacher Slice.

tin for 5 minutes before turning onto wire rack to cool.

6. To make Icing: Place chocolate, butter and liqueur in medium heatproof bowl. Stand over pan of simmering water, stir until chocolate has melted and mixture is smooth. Cool for 10–15 minutes or until icing is thick enough to spread evenly over cake, using a flat-bladed knife. Refrigerate for 30 minutes before transferring to plate for serving.

Note: Sacher Slice can be split in the middle and spread with apricot or plum jam. It is also good as a dessert, with cream or ice-cream. It can be stored, in an airtight container, for two to three days in a cool, dry place.

Morsels

For morning coffee, a church supper or more casual get-together, you'll find these easy-to-handle sweet tastes just the thing. They're ideal for fêtes and cake stalls, too, and if there should be any leftovers, they will prove a popular addition to school lunchboxes.

Pithiviers

Preparation time:
  20 minutes
Total cooking time:
  20 minutes
Makes one 23 cm round

2 *sheets ready-rolled puff pastry*
1 *egg, lightly beaten*
1 *tablespoon icing sugar*

Filling
90 *g butter*
2/3 *cup icing sugar, extra*
2 *egg yolks*
1 1/4 *cups ground almonds*
2 *teaspoons almond essence*

1. Preheat oven to moderately hot 210°C (gas 190°C). Brush a 32 x 28 cm oven tray with melted butter or oil. Using a cake tin as a guide, cut a 23 cm round from one sheet of pastry and a 25 cm round from the other. Place the 23 cm round onto oven tray.
2. *To make Filling:* Using electric beaters, beat butter and extra icing sugar in medium mixing bowl until light and creamy. Add egg yolks, beat until combined. Add almonds and essence, stir until combined.
3. Spread filling over pastry base, leaving a 2.5 cm border. Place remaining pastry round over top; press slightly on border to seal.
4. Mark into eight curved wedges, being careful not to cut all the way through. Make deep cuts around the border at 2 cm intervals.
5. Brush pastry all over with combined beaten egg and icing sugar. Bake for 20 minutes or until puffed and golden.

From top: Lamingtons and Fruit Tartlets (page 28) and Pithiviers.

Fruit Tartlets

Preparation time:
  20 minutes
Total cooking time:
  40 minutes
Makes 12

12 frozen (unbaked)
  shortcrust pastry
  tartlet cases
2 tablespoons custard
  powder
1/3 cup cornflour
1/3 cup caster sugar
1 teaspoon vanilla essence
2 egg yolks
1 1/4 cups cream
2/3 cup milk
12 strawberries
200 g punnet blueberries

Glaze
1 tablespoon apricot jam
2 tablespoons orange
  juice
2 teaspoons gelatine

1. Preheat oven to
moderate 180°C. Place
frozen tartlets in foil
cases on oven tray.
Bake 25 minutes or
until golden and
cooked through. Cool.
2. Place custard powder,
cornflour, sugar, essence
and yolks into medium
mixing bowl. Whisk
together until mixture is
smooth and pale. Heat
cream and milk in pan
until almost boiling;
remove from heat.
3. Add milk gradually to
custard mixture,
whisking constantly.

Strain mixture into pan.
Stir constantly with a
wooden spoon over
medium heat 8 minutes
or until custard boils
and thickens. Remove
from heat. Place plastic
wrap over custard
surface; cool.
4. Divide custard
mixture evenly between
the tart cases. Using a
flat-bladed knife, shape
mixture into a mound;
smooth surface.
Decorate with fruit.
Brush thickly with glaze.
5. *To make Glaze:*
Combine jam, juice and
gelatine in small pan. Stir
over low heat 2 minutes
or until gelatine dissolves
and mixture boils.
Remove from heat;
strain, cool slightly.

Lamingtons

Preparation time:
  1 hour
Total cooking time:
  30 minutes
Makes 16 lamingtons

1 cup self-raising flour
4 eggs
3/4 cup sugar
1/3 cup milk
30 g butter

Icing
4 cups (500 g) icing
  sugar, sifted
1/2 cup cocoa powder
1/2 cup water
4 cups (500 g) desiccated
  coconut

1. Preheat oven to
moderate 180°C. Brush
a 30 x 20 cm shallow
rectangular cake tin
with melted butter or
oil. Line base and two
sides with paper; grease
paper. Sift flour three
times onto greaseproof
paper.
2. Using electric
beaters, beat eggs in
small mixing bowl for
10 minutes or until
thick and pale. Add
sugar gradually, beating
constantly until
dissolved and mixture
is pale yellow and
glossy. Transfer mixture
to large bowl.
3. Place milk and butter
in small pan. Heat over
low heat until butter is
melted.
4. Using large metal
spoon, fold flour into
egg mixture quickly and
lightly. Fold in hot milk
and butter.
5. Spread mixture
evenly into prepared
tin. Bake for 30 minutes
or until cake is lightly
golden and shrinks
away from side of tin.
Stand cake in tin for
5 minutes before
turning out on wire
rack to cool.
6. Carefully trim outer
edges of cake and cut
into 16 even pieces.
7. *To make Icing:*
Combine sifted icing
sugar and cocoa
and sufficient liquid
in a medium bowl to
form a firm paste.

Banana and Raisin Muffins.

Stand bowl over pan of simmering water, stirring until icing is smooth and glossy; remove from heat.
8. Dip each piece of cake into icing and hold over bowl to allow excess icing to drain back into bowl. Place immediately into bowl of coconut and toss gently to ensure cake is completely covered. Stand on wire rack for 20 minutes or until icing is dry.

Note: It is best to make the lamington cake the day before cutting and icing it.

Banana and Raisin Muffins

Preparation time:
  15 minutes
Total cooking time:
  15 minutes
Makes 18

2 *cups self-raising flour*
1 *cup oatbran* 403
3/4 *cup caster sugar* 60?
125 *g butter, melted*
1 *cup milk*
2 *eggs, lightly beaten*
1 *cup (2 medium)*
  mashed, ripe banana
1/3 *cup chopped*
  raisins

1. Preheat oven to moderately hot 210°C (gas 190°C). Brush oil into 18 muffin cups (1/3 cup capacity) . Sift flour into mixing bowl. Add oatbran and sugar. Make well in centre.
2. Combine butter, milk, eggs, banana and raisins in a small bowl. Add to dry ingredients all at once. Using a wooden spoon, stir until just mixed; do not overbeat.
3. Spoon mixture into prepared muffin tin, filling two-thirds full. Bake for 15 minutes or until puffed and golden brown. Turn onto wire rack to cool.

29

Cream Horns

Preparation time:
  20 minutes
Total cooking time:
  30 minutes
Makes 8

375 g block puff pastry
1 egg white, lightly
  beaten
1 tablespoon caster
  sugar
1/4 cup strawberry jam

Custard Cream
1/2 cup full cream milk
  powder
1/4 cup caster sugar
1/4 cup custard powder
1 1/4 cups water
1/3 cup cream

1. Preheat oven to hot
240°C (gas 200°C).
Line two 32 x 28 cm
biscuit trays with
baking paper. Brush
eight cream horn
moulds with melted
butter or oil.
2. Roll pastry on lightly
floured surface to
50 x 20 cm rectangle.
Using a sharp knife, cut
pastry lengthways into
eight 2.5 cm-wide strips.
3. Beginning at the
narrow end of mould,
wrap a strip of pastry
over the mould,
overlapping slightly
each time until you
reach the end. Brush the
pastry lightly with the
egg white; sprinkle with
sugar. Place onto

prepared tray. Repeat
process with remaining
pastry.
4. Bake 20 minutes.
Reduce heat to 210°C
(gas 190°C), bake
further 10 minutes or
until well browned and
puffed. Leave horns on
trays for 5 minutes.
Carefully twist to
remove moulds from
horns. Transfer horns to
wire rack to cool.
5. *To make Custard
Cream:* Place milk
powder, sugar and
custard powder into
small pan. Gradually
add water, blend with a
whisk until smooth.
Whisk over low heat
10 minutes or until
mixture boils and
thickens; remove from
heat. Cover with plastic
wrap; cool. Transfer
mixture to small mixing
bowl. Using electric
beaters, beat custard
and cream on medium
speed 1 minute or until
mixture is thick and
creamy. Custard cream
can be made one day
ahead. Store, covered
with plastic wrap, in
refrigerator. To
assemble, place one
teaspoon jam into base
of each horn. Fill horns
with custard cream.

Vienna Swirls

Preparation time:
  20 minutes
Total cooking time:
  15 minutes
Makes about 20

125 g butter, softened
1/4 cup sour cream
1/2 cup icing sugar
1/2 teaspoon vanilla
  essence
1 cup plain flour
1/4 cup rice flour

1. Preheat oven to
moderate 180°C. Line
two deep patty tins
with paper patty cases.
Using electric beaters,
beat the butter, sour
cream, sifted icing
sugar and vanilla in
a small mixing bowl
until mixture is light
and creamy.
2. Add sifted flour and
rice flour, stir until
combined.
3. Spoon mixture into a
piping bag fitted with a
fluted piping nozzle;
pipe mixture into
prepared patty cases to
one-third full. Bake for
15 minutes or until
swirls are lightly
golden.

Note: A small piece of
glacé cherry can be
placed on the top of
each swirl before
baking.

Vienna Swirls (top) and Cream Horns.

Add water to flour and butter mixture, stir with knife until just combined.

Roll dough into a rectangle, fold one end over the other; repeat five times.

Passionfruit Palmiers

Preparation time:
  30 minutes
Total cooking time:
  15 minutes
Makes about 25

2 cups plain flour
1 teaspoon baking
  powder
185 g cold butter,
  chopped
1/2 cup water
1 tablespoon sugar

Passionfruit Icing
1 1/2 cups icing sugar
30 g butter, melted
2 passionfruit

1. Preheat oven to moderately hot 210°C (gas 190°C). Line two 32 x 28 cm biscuit trays with baking paper. Sift flour and baking powder into a large mixing bowl.

Add butter, stir until combined. Add water, stir with a knife until just combined. Turn onto lightly floured surface, knead for 1 minute or until smooth. **2.** Roll dough to a rectangle approximately 40 x 20 cm. With the short end towards you, fold the end over to two-thirds of the way along the rectangle. Fold the other end back over the top. Turn dough clockwise so the open end is towards you. **3.** Roll dough to a rectangle, fold and turn dough as above, five more times. If butter becomes soft, refrigerate dough for 30 minutes, being sure to continue rolling and folding in the same direction.

4. Roll dough on lightly floured surface to a 32 x 30 cm rectangle, trim. Sprinkle with sugar. Fold the long sides to meet in the centre. Fold in half lengthways. **5.** Using a sharp knife, cut into 1 cm slices. Lay slices cut side up on prepared trays; open slices out slightly, brush lightly with water. Bake for 15 minutes or until lightly golden. Transfer to wire rack to cool. **6.** *To make Passionfruit Icing:* Sift icing sugar into a medium mixing bowl, add butter and passionfruit pulp, stir until combined. Spread icing over palmiers.

Note: Be sure to roll, fold and turn the pastry the same way each time so that the layers will all run in the same direction and therefore give a light and crisp result. Store for two days in an airtight container.

Passionfruit Palmiers.

Fold the long sides of dough to meet centre. Fold in half lengthways.

To make icing, combine icing sugar, butter and passionfruit pulp.

Mini Fruit Danish

Preparation time:
  40 minutes
Total cooking time:
  15 minutes
Makes 18

2 sheets puff pastry
1/2 cup apricot jam,
  strained
1 tablespoon water

Apricot Filling
30 g butter, softened
1/4 cup icing sugar
1 egg yolk
1/4 cup ground almonds
425 g can apricot
  halves, drained

1. Preheat oven to moderately hot 210°C (gas 190°C). Brush two 32 x 28 cm biscuit trays with melted butter or oil. Cut each pastry sheet into three strips. Cut each of the strips into three, to give 18 squares.

2. **To make Apricot Filling:** Beat butter and icing sugar in small bowl, with wooden spoon, until smooth. Add egg yolk and almonds, beat until combined.

3. Divide filling between the pastry squares, spread slightly.

Place two apricot halves diagonally onto each square. Bring the remaining two corners of each square over the apricots, press the corners together.

4. Place onto biscuit trays. Bake 15 minutes or until golden brown; remove from oven.

5. Brush with combined jam and water, allow to cool before serving.

Custard Tarts

Preparation time:
 30 minutes + 20
 minutes refrigeration
Total cooking time:
 45 minutes
Makes twelve 10 cm
tarts

2 cups plain flour
1/3 cup rice flour
1/4 cup icing sugar
120 g butter
1 egg yolk
1/4 cup iced water
1 egg white, lightly
 beaten

Filling
3 eggs
1 1/2 cups milk
1/4 cup caster sugar
1 teaspoon vanilla
 essence
1/2 teaspoon nutmeg

1. Place flours, icing sugar and butter in food processor bowl. Using the pulse action, press the button for 20 seconds or until the mixture is fine and crumbly. Add egg yolk and almost all water, process 30 seconds or until mixture comes together, adding more water if necessary. Turn onto a lightly floured surface, press together until smooth. Divide dough into 12 equal portions, roll out and line twelve 10 cm fluted tart tins. Refrigerate 20 minutes.

2. Preheat oven to moderate 180°C. Cut sheets of greaseproof paper to cover each pastry-lined tin. Spread a layer of dried beans or rice evenly over paper. Place tart tins on a large flat baking tray and bake 10 minutes. Remove from oven; discard baking paper and beans/rice. Return to oven and bake a further 10 minutes or until lightly golden. Cool. Brush base and sides of each pastry case with beaten egg white.

3. *To make Filling:* Reduce oven to low 150°C. Combine eggs and milk in a medium mixing bowl, whisk to combine. Add sugar gradually, whisking to dissolve completely. Stir in essence. Strain mixture into a jug, then pour into pastry cases. Sprinkle with nutmeg and bake for 25 minutes or until filling is just set. Serve tarts at room temperature.

Notes: Be careful not to overcook the tarts as the eggs in the filling will curdle. Ground cinnamon can be used instead of nutmeg.

Custard Tarts (left) and Mini Fruit Danish.

Shortbread

Preparation time:
  20 minutes
Total cooking time:
  35–40 minutes
Makes 24 pieces

250 g butter
3/4 cup caster sugar
2 cups plain flour
1/2 cup cornflour

1. Preheat oven to
moderately slow 160°C.
Brush a 28 x 18 cm
shallow rectangular
cake tin with melted
butter or oil. Cover base
with paper; extending
over sides; grease paper.
2. Beat butter and sugar
in small mixing bowl
with electric beaters
until light and creamy.
3. Add sifted flours,
press together to form a
soft dough. Turn onto a
lightly floured surface;
knead lightly until
smooth. Press dough
into prepared tin.
4. Score into fingers.
Pierce with fork. Bake
for 35–40 minutes or
until set and browned.
When almost cool cut
through lines into
pieces.

Note: Dough can be
rolled out and cut into
small rounds or bars.
Adjust cooking to suit.

Neenish Tarts

Preparation time:
  25 minutes
Total cooking time:
  Nil
Makes 12

Buttercream
60 g unsalted butter
1/2 cup icing sugar,
  sifted
1 tablespoon milk
few drops imitation
  rum essence

12 precooked tartlet
  cases
2 tablespoons raspberry
  jam
1 cup icing sugar, extra
1 teaspoon vanilla essence
3 teaspoons hot water
few drops pink food
  colouring

1. Place butter into
small mixing bowl.
Using electric beaters,
beat on high speed for
1 minute. Add sugar,
milk and essence, beat
until light and creamy.
2. Place 1/2 teaspoon
jam into each tartlet;
spread over base. Top
jam with 2 teaspoons
buttercream mixture;
smooth surface with
back of a teaspoon.

*From top: Shortbread, Coffee Meringue Kisses
and Neenish Tarts.*

3. Sift icing sugar into
small mixing bowl;
make a well in centre.
Add essence and water.
Using a flat-bladed
knife stir until mixture
is smooth. Divide
mixture into two
portions. Leave one
portion plain and
tint the remaining
portion pink.
4. Spread 1 teaspoon
plain icing over half of
each tartlet; allow to
set. Spread 1 teaspoon
pink icing over
remaining half of each
tartlet; allow to set.

Coffee Meringue Kisses

Preparation time:
  20 minutes
Total cooking time:
  30 minutes
Makes about 24

3 egg whites
3/4 cup caster sugar
cocoa powder for dusting

Filling
125 g cream cheese
1/2 cup icing sugar
2 teaspoons instant
  coffee powder
2 teaspoons hot water

1. Preheat oven to
slow 150°C. Line two
32 x 28 cm oven trays
with baking paper.
2 Place egg whites in a
small, dry mixing bowl.

Using electric beaters, beat egg whites until firm peaks form. Add sugar gradually, beating constantly until mixture is thick and glossy and all sugar is dissolved.

3. Spoon mixture into a piping bag fitted with a fluted piping nozzle. Pipe meringue onto trays, in mounds about 2 cm in diameter.

4. Bake for 30 minutes or until meringues are pale and crisp. Cool completely in the oven, with door slightly ajar.

5. *To make Filling:* Beat cream cheese and icing sugar until light and creamy. Combine coffee and water, stir until dissolved; add to mixture, beat until combined.

6. Spread the base of a meringue with a little filling; join together with another meringue. Repeat with remaining meringues and filling. Dust with cocoa powder if desired.

HINT

Store meringues in a cool, dark place in an airtight container for up to three days. Fill just before serving. Test that the meringues are dry inside before turning off the oven. If not dry, they will become soft on standing. Soft meringues can be re-crisped in a cool oven.

Bakewell Slice

Preparation time:
  30 minutes
Total cooking time:
  25 minutes
Makes 18

1 cup plain flour
90 g butter
1 tablespoon caster
  sugar
1 tablespoon water
1/2 cup raspberry jam
1/4 cup flaked almonds

Topping
185 g butter, extra
3/4 cup caster sugar,
  extra
3 eggs, lightly beaten
1 cup ground almonds
3/4 cup plain flour, extra

1. Preheat oven to moderately hot 210°C (gas 190°C). Brush a shallow 28 x 18 x 3 cm rectangular cake tin with melted butter or oil. Cover base with paper, extending over two sides; grease paper.

2. Place sifted flour, butter and sugar into a food processor bowl. Using pulse action, press button for 10 seconds or until mixture is fine and crumbly. Add water, process 5 seconds until mixture is smooth.

3. Turn mixture into prepared tin, press evenly over base using lightly floured hands.

Bake for 5 minutes, remove from oven, allow to cool.

4. *To make Topping:* Using electric beaters, beat extra butter and sugar in small mixing bowl until light and creamy. Add eggs gradually, beating thoroughly after each addition. Transfer mixture to large mixing bowl; add almonds and extra flour. Using a wooden spoon, stir until just combined.

5. Spread pastry base evenly with jam. Spread evenly with topping, sprinkle with almonds. Bake for 20 minutes or until lightly golden, cool in tin. Cut into fingers when cold.

Chocolate Eclairs

Preparation time:
  40 minutes
Total cooking time:
  27 minutes
Makes 10–12 eclairs

40 g butter
1/2 cup water
1/2 cup plain flour
2 eggs
11/4 cream, whipped
125 g dark chocolate,
  chopped
20 g butter

1. Preheat oven to moderately hot 210°C (gas 190°C). Brush a 32 x 28 cm oven tray

38

Chocolate Eclairs (top) and Bakewell Slice.

with melted butter or oil. Combine butter and water in medium pan. Stir over low heat until butter has melted; do not boil. Remove from heat, add flour all at once. Beat until smooth using a wooden spoon. Return to stove, heat until mixture thickens and comes away from side and base of pan. Remove from heat; cool slightly.

2. Transfer mixture to large mixer bowl. Add beaten eggs gradually, beating until mixture is glossy.

3. Spoon mixture into piping bag fitted with small plain pipe. Pipe mixture in 8 cm lengths, 5 cm apart on prepared tray. Bake for 12 minutes. Reduce heat to moderate 180°C. Bake a further 15 minutes or until crisp and brown.

4. Cut eclairs in half lengthways, remove any uncooked mixture.

Return puffs to oven for 4 minutes or until dry. Cool on wire rack.

5. Fill each eclair base with whipped cream, replace tops. Spread each eclair with melted chocolate.

6. *To melt chocolate:* Place chocolate and butter in small heatproof bowl. Stand over pan of simmering water, stir until chocolate has melted and mixture is smooth. Cool slightly.

Stir butter, syrup and sugar over low heat until butter has melted.

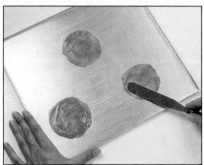

Place teaspoons of mixture on tray, smooth to 8 cm rounds.

Brandy Snap Fans

Preparation time:
 45 minutes
Total cooking time:
 4 minutes each batch
Makes 20

30 g unsalted butter
2 tablespoons golden
 syrup
1 tablespoon soft
 brown sugar
2 tablespoons plain
 flour, sifted
1 teaspoon ground
 ginger
60 g dark chocolate,
 melted

1. Preheat oven to moderate 180°C. Brush a 32 x 28 cm oven tray with melted butter or oil.
2. Combine butter, golden syrup and sugar in small pan. Stir over low heat until butter has just melted and mixture is smooth; do not boil.
3. Remove pan from heat. Transfer mixture to small bowl. Add flour and ginger. Stir with a wooden spoon until just combined; do not overbeat.
4. Place a level teaspoon of mixture at a time onto prepared tray. Using a flat-bladed knife, spread mixture to make an 8 cm round. (Do not cook more than three at a time). Bake 4 minutes or until bubbling and lightly browned. Remove tray from oven. Leave rounds on tray for 20 seconds. Carefully loosen edges.
5. Lift round from tray. Beginning from one side of round, quickly pleat or fold towards opposite side in palm of your hand. Pinch folds together at one end to resemble a fan. Repeat process quickly with remaining rounds. Allow to set. Repeat baking and fanning process with remaining mixture.
6. Place melted chocolate into a small bowl. Dip end of fans into chocolate. Allow to set on wire rack.

HINTS
Do not cook more than three rounds at a time; shaping can become difficult as they begin to cool. Instead of making fans, the cooked rounds can be pinched or gathered across the centre to resemble a bow if preferred.

Brandy Snap Fans.

Pinch folds of cooked round together at one end to make a fan.

Dip open ends of cooled fans into melted chocolate. Allow to set.

41

Madeleines

Preparation time:
  20 minutes
Total cooking time:
  10–15 minutes
Makes 12

1 cup plain flour
2 eggs
3/4 cup sugar
185 g unsalted butter,
  melted and cooled
1 teaspoon finely grated
  lemon rind
1/3 cup icing sugar

1. Preheat oven to moderate 180°C. Brush madeleine tins with melted butter or oil. Dust tins with flour; shake off excess. Sift flour three times onto greaseproof paper.
2. Combine eggs and sugar in heatproof bowl. Place bowl over pan of simmering water. Beat until mixture is thick and pale yellow. Remove from heat, continue to beat until cooled slightly and increased in volume.
3. Add flour, butter and rind. Using a metal spoon, fold quickly and lightly until ingredients are just combined.
4. Spoon mixture carefully into prepared moulds. Bake for 10–12 minutes. Remove from tins; place on wire rack until cold. Dust with icing sugar.

Hint

Madeleine tins are available from specialty kitchenware shops. Shallow patty tins may be used instead.

Apple Kuchen Slice

Preparation time:
  20 minutes + 20
  minutes refrigeration
Total cooking time:
  50 minutes
Makes 12 pieces

1 1/3 cups plain flour
125 g butter, chopped
1 tablespoon caster sugar
1 egg yolk
3 medium green apples,
  peeled and thinly sliced
2 tablespoons caster
  sugar
3 teaspoons lemon juice
1/2 teaspoon ground
  cinnamon
cinnamon sugar

Topping
1 1/4 cups sour cream
2 tablespoons caster
  sugar
1 teaspoon vanilla
  essence
2 eggs, lightly beaten

1. Preheat oven to moderate 180°C. Brush a 30 x 20 cm shallow rectangular cake tin with melted butter or oil. Cover base with paper, extending over two sides; grease paper. Place flour in food processor bowl; add butter and sugar.
2. Using the pulse action, press button for 30 seconds or until mixture is fine and crumbly. Add egg yolk to bowl. Process 10 seconds or until mixture comes together.
3. Press mixture into prepared tin with the back of a spoon; smooth surface. Cover with plastic wrap, refrigerate 20 minutes. Bake pastry 15 minutes. Remove from oven; cool.
4. Place apples, sugar, juice and cinnamon in large bowl; mix well. Arrange apples in overlapping rows over pastry base. Bake 15 minutes. Remove from oven.
To make Topping: Place cream in medium mixing bowl. Beat with a wire whisk until smooth. Add sugar, vanilla and eggs, whisk until well combined. Pour topping over apples; return to oven. Bake further 20 minutes or until topping is set. Cool in tin. Sprinkle with cinnamon sugar before serving. Cut into 12 fingers/bars or diamonds.

Apple Kuchen Slice (top) and Madeleines.

44

Coconut Almond Macaroons

Preparation time:
20 minutes
Total cooking time:
30 minutes
Makes 30

2 eggs, separated
2/3 cup caster sugar
1/2 teaspoon cream of
  tartar
1 teaspoon vanilla
  essence
1 1/2 cup desiccated
  coconut
1 cup flaked almonds

1. Preheat oven to moderately slow 160°C. Line a 32 x 18 cm biscuit tray with baking paper. Place egg whites in a small dry mixing bowl. Using electric beaters, beat the egg whites until firm peaks form.
2. Add sugar gradually, beating constantly until mixture is thick and glossy and all the sugar is dissolved.
3. Fold in cream of tartar, vanilla essence, coconut and almonds. Drop teaspoonsful of the mixture onto prepared trays.
4. Bake for 30 minutes or until crisp. Loosen and allow to cool on trays.

Caramel Nut Tartlets

Preparation time:
30 minutes
Total cooking time:
30 minutes
Makes about 18

3/4 cup plain flour
1 tablespoon caster
  sugar
45 g butter
1 tablespoon milk

Filling
250 g unsalted whole
  nut mix
1/2 cup sugar
1/4 cup water
1/4 cup cream

1. Preheat oven to moderate 180°C. Sift flour into a medium mixing bowl; add sugar and chopped butter. Using fingertips, rub butter into flour for 2 minutes or until mixture is fine and crumbly, stir in milk and mix to a soft dough. Turn onto lightly floured surface, knead for 1 minute or until smooth.
2. Roll pastry thinly, cut into circles using a 6 cm fluted round cutter. Press pastry circles into greased shallow patty tins. Prick evenly with a fork. Bake for 10 minutes or until lightly golden.
3. **To make Filling:** Spread nuts onto an oven tray. Bake for 10 minutes or until lightly golden. Combine sugar and water in a medium pan. Stir constantly over low heat until sugar has dissolved. Bring to boil. Reduce heat, simmer uncovered, without stirring, for 10 minutes or until golden brown. Remove from heat, add cream, stir until combined. (If the syrup sets in lumps when the cream is added, return pan to the heat for 1 minute or until mixture becomes smooth.) Add nuts, stir until combined.
4. Spoon hot filling into pastry shells, allow to cool before serving.

> **HINT**
> The sugar and water syrup should be a medium golden colour when cooked. If it is too pale, the filling will not set. If it becomes too dark, it will burn. Cook syrup over a low heat. Remove pan during the cooking process to check if the syrup is ready.

Coconut Almond Macaroons (top)
and Caramel Nut Tartlets.

Cinnamon Fritters

Preparation time:
  10 minutes
Total cooking time:
  3 minutes per batch
Makes about 24

1 cup water
60 g butter
2 tablespoons caster
  sugar
1 cup self-raising flour
4 eggs
oil for deep frying
2 tablespoons icing
  sugar
1 teaspoon ground
  cinnamon

1. Combine water, butter and caster sugar in a medium pan. Stir over low heat for 1 minute or until butter has melted; do not boil.
2. Remove pan from heat, add flour all at once. Using a wooden spoon, beat until smooth. Return to stove, heat until mixture thickens and comes away from side and base of pan. Remove from heat; cool slightly.
3. Transfer mixture to large mixing bowl. Using electric beaters, add eggs gradually, beating until mixture is glossy and thick.
4. Heat oil in a deep heavy-based pan over medium heat. Gently lower level tablespoons of mixture into oil in small batches. Cook over medium heat for 3 minutes or until golden brown and puffed. Carefully remove from oil with a slotted spoon. Drain on paper towel. Repeat with remaining mixture.
5. Place fritters on serving plate, dust with combined icing sugar and cinnamon. Serve immediately.

Cheese and Pear Danish

Preparation time:
  20 minutes
Total cooking time:
  23 minutes
Makes 8

425 g can pear halves
  in natural juice
250 g cream cheese,
  softened
2 tablespoons caster
  sugar
1 teaspoon cornflour
1 egg
2 teaspoons vanilla
  essence
2 sheets ready-rolled
  butter puff pastry
2 tablespoons sugar
1 tablespoon gelatine

1. Preheat oven to hot 240°C (gas 200°C). Line two 32 x 28 cm oven trays with baking paper. Drain pears well; reserve one-third cup juice for glaze. Cut each pear half into thin slices.
2. Place cheese, sugar, cornflour, egg and essence into small mixing bowl. Using electric beaters, beat on medium speed for 3 minutes or until mixture is creamy and smooth.
3. Cut each pastry sheet evenly into four squares. Place two heaped tablespoons cheese mixture diagonally across centre of each pastry square. Overlap about three slices of pear onto cheese mixture at each end.
4. Carefully fold opposite ends of pastry over to enclose cheese filling; press to seal. Place on prepared trays. Bake 20 minutes or until well puffed and lightly browned. Remove from oven, transfer to wire rack to cool.
5. Combine reserved pear juice, sugar and gelatine in small pan. Stir over low heat for 3 minutes or until sugar dissolves and mixture boils. Remove from heat; cool slightly. Brush cooled danish liberally with glaze. Allow glaze to set before serving.

*Cinnamon Fritters (top)
and Cheese and Pear Danish.*

Nut and Meringue Fingers

Preparation time:
  40 minutes
Total cooking time:
  30–35 minutes
Makes 16 pieces

125 g butter
1/2 cup caster sugar
1 egg
1 1/2 cups self-raising
  flour

Topping
1/2 cup apricot jam
3 egg whites
1/2 cup sugar
1/2 cup (60 g) finely
  chopped pecans
1/3 cup (60 g) finely
  chopped almonds

1. Preheat oven to moderate 180°C. Brush a shallow rectangular 30 x 20 cm cake tin with melted butter or oil. Line base and two sides with paper.

2. Using electric beaters, beat butter and sugar in small mixing bowl until light and creamy. Add egg gradually, beating well after each addition.
3. Transfer mixture to large mixing bowl. Using a metal spoon fold in sifted flour, stir until just combined and the mixture is almost smooth. Press mixture evenly into prepared tin; smooth surface.

Prune, Apple and Almond Slice (left) and Nut and Meringue Fingers.

5. Bake for 30–35 minutes or until pastry is cooked and meringue set. Allow to cool before cutting into fingers.

Prune, Apple and Almond Slice

Preparation time:
 40 minutes
Total cooking time:
 1 hour
Makes 23 cm round

100 g unsalted butter
1/3 cup caster sugar
2 eggs
3/4 cup plain flour, sifted
375 g fresh ricotta cheese
1 teaspoon grated lime rind
1/3 cup caster sugar
2 eggs
1/3 cup chopped prunes
2 tablespoons cornflour
410 g can pie apple
1 1/4 cups flaked almonds, toasted

1. Preheat oven to moderate 180°C. Brush a 23 cm round springform tin with melted butter or oil, line base with paper; grease paper.
2. Using electric beaters, beat butter and sugar in small mixing bowl until light and creamy. Add eggs gradually, beating thoroughly after each addition. Add flour. Using a flat-bladed knife, mix to a thick paste. Spread/press mixture evenly over base of prepared tin. Bake for 15 minutes.
3. Place cheese, rind and sugar in small mixing bowl. Using electric beaters, beat until creamy. Add eggs gradually, beating thoroughly after each addition. Add prunes and cornflour; beat until just combined. Transfer mixture to large mixing bowl.
4. Using a metal spoon, fold in the apple and half the almonds. Stir until just combined. Spoon mixture over pre-cooked base; smooth surface.
5. Scatter remaining almonds over cheese mixture; press gently onto surface. Bake for 45 minutes or until the filling is firm and golden. Cool in tin. To serve, cut into wedges. This slice is best stored in the refrigerator.

Note: You could substitute one-third cup fresh raspberries or blueberries for the prunes, if preferred.

4. *To make Topping:* Spread pastry base evenly with jam. Place egg whites in small dry mixing bowl. Using electric beaters, beat egg whites until firm peaks form. Add sugar gradually, beating constantly until mixture is thick and glossy and all the sugar is dissolved. Carefully fold in nuts. Spread meringue mixture evenly over jam.

Honey Nut Strudel

Preparation time:
40 minutes
Total cooking time:
35 minutes
Serves 6–8

250 g cream cheese,
softened
2 egg yolks
2 tablespoons caster
sugar
2 tablespoons honey
1/2 teaspoon ground
cloves
21/2 cups (300 g)
chopped walnuts
1 cup (120 g) ground
almonds
90 g butter, melted
10 sheets filo pastry

Honey Syrup
1/3 cup honey
2 tablespoons water
1 tablespoon lemon
juice
1 teaspoon grated
lemon rind
5 whole cloves

1. Preheat oven to
moderately hot 210°C
(gas 190°C). Brush a
deep, 20 cm round
springform tin with
melted butter or oil,
line base with paper;
grease paper. Place
cheese, yolks, sugar and
honey into small mixing
bowl. Using electric
beaters, beat 3 minutes
on high speed until
light and creamy. Add
cloves and nuts; stir

with a metal spoon
until just combined.
2. Place five sheets of
pastry onto work
surface. Keep remaining
sheets covered with a
damp cloth to prevent
sheets drying out. Brush
each sheet of pastry all
over with butter. Top
with second sheet of
pastry. Repeat process
until five sheets have
been layered. Do not
brush top sheet with
butter. Cover and set
aside. Repeat process
with remaining five
sheets of pastry.
3. Lay the two lots of
pastry lengthways
across work surface.
Brush along narrow
end of one lot of pastry
with butter. Carefully
overlap second lot of
pastry about 10 cm
onto buttered end.
(Pastry should now be
about 60 cm long.)
4. Spoon creamy nut
mixture evenly along
edge of pastry closest to
you, leaving a 10 cm
border at each end.
Roll pastry over to
enclose filling. Fold
ends over to seal in
filling. Complete rolling
to end of pastry. Brush
all over with remaining
butter.
5. Beginning at one
end, carefully roll the
pastry into a spiral,
large enough to fit the
tin. Place into prepared
tin, bake 30 minutes or
until well browned and

crisp. Pour cooled
syrup over hot roll.
Cool in tin.
6. *To make Honey
Syrup:* Combine all
ingredients in small
pan. Stir over low heat
until mixture boils.
Simmer, uncovered,
without stirring, for
5 minutes.

Apricot Coconut Crescents

Preparation time:
40 minutes
Total cooking time:
50 minutes
Makes 16

11/2 cups (200 g)
chopped dried apricots
3/4 cup water
1 tablespoon butter
1/2 cup condensed milk
1/2 cup desiccated
coconut
1/2 teaspoon grated
lime rind
4 sheets ready-rolled
shortcrust pastry
1 egg white, lightly
beaten
1/4 cup desiccated
coconut, extra

1. Preheat oven to
moderate 180°C. Line a
32 x 28 cm oven tray
with baking paper.
Place the apricots,
water and butter in
small pan. Stir over
medium heat 3 minutes
or until mixture boils.

Honey Nut Strudel (left) and Apricot Coconut Crescents.

Reduce heat, simmer uncovered, 12 minutes or until mixture is thick and almost all liquid is absorbed.
2. Add the milk, stir over low heat for 5 minutes. Remove from heat, add coconut and rind. Stir to combine; cool. Cut each

pastry sheet evenly into four squares. Spread 1 tablespoon of mixture over a square, leaving one corner uncovered.
3. Roll opposite corner towards the uncovered corner of pastry, shape into a crescent. Repeat process with remaining pastry and filling.

4. Arrange crescents onto prepared tray about 3 cm apart; brush with egg white. Sprinkle crescents with coconut. Bake for 25 minutes or until golden and cooked through. Leave on tray 5 minutes before transferring to wire rack.

51

Savoury

These scrumptious savouries will do double duty – they're perfect at afternoon tea time, and will be equally at home with cocktails or pre-dinner drinks, as a first course for a dinner party or, served with a green salad, as a light lunch.

Sandwiches

Preparation time:
  35 minutes
Total cooking time:
  Nil
Serves 4–6

PINWHEEL SANDWICHES
1 loaf unsliced white or
  brown bread

Filling
250 g cream cheese,
  softened
1/2 cup (90 g) finely
  chopped dates
3/4 cup (90 g) finely
  chopped walnuts
1 teaspoon finely grated
  orange rind

1. Cut crusts from loaf. Cut loaf lengthways into slices.
2. Combine cheese, dates, walnuts and orange rind.
3. Spread filling evenly onto each slice; roll up from either long or short side of bread. Wrap tightly in plastic wrap and refrigerate for 1 hour.
4. Slice into rounds using a serrated knife.

FINGER SANDWICHES
1/2 loaf white sliced
  bread
1 loaf wholemeal
  bread
250 g unsalted butter,
  creamed

Filling 1
250 g can red salmon,
  drained, skin and
  bones removed
1 tablespoon
  mayonnaise
1 teaspoon lemon
  juice
1/2 teaspoon freshly
  ground black pepper

Filling 2
2 Lebanese cucumbers,
  peeled and thinly sliced
1 teaspoon finely grated
  lemon rind

Pinwheel and Finger Sandwiches and Chive and Onion Scones with Bacon Butter (page 54).

1. Butter the white bread on both sides, wholemeal bread on one side only.
2. Combine salmon, mayonnaise, juice and pepper.
3. Place half of the wholemeal bread slices on a large flat surface. Spread evenly with salmon mixture. Top with white slices. Top with cucumber and lemon rind and finish with remaining wholemeal slices.
4. Using a serrated knife, remove crusts from sandwiches. Cut each sandwich into three fingers.

Note: Sandwiches are best made close to serving time. If necessary, they can be covered with plastic wrap and stored in the refrigerator for up to two hours.

Chive and Onion Scones with Bacon Butter

Preparation time:
  12 minutes
Total cooking time:
  25 minutes
Makes 32 pieces

Bacon Butter
90 g butter, softened
2 teaspoons bacon chips

Chive and Onion Scones

3 cups self-raising flour
40 g sachet French onion soup mix
60 g butter
1 cup milk
1 egg yolk
2 tablespoons freshly chopped chives
2 tablespoons milk, extra

1. Preheat oven to hot 240°C (gas 200°C). Line a 32 x 28 cm oven tray with baking paper.
To make Bacon Butter: Combine butter and bacon chips in small bowl; mix well. Store, covered with plastic wrap in refrigerator, 30 minutes.
2. Place flour, soup mix and butter in food processor bowl. Using the pulse action, press button for 15 seconds. Add milk, yolk and chives to bowl, process 5 seconds or until mixture almost forms a dough.
3. Turn dough onto lightly floured surface; knead for 30 seconds. Press mixture evenly into a floured shallow 30 x 20 cm rectangular tin. Turn out onto a floured board. Using a sharp knife, cut dough

into 32 pieces. Brush tops with extra milk.
4. Arrange pieces evenly apart onto prepared oven tray. Bake for 10 minutes. Reduce temperature to moderately hot 210°C (gas 190°C), and bake a further 15 minutes or until well risen and browned. Serve warm with chilled bacon butter.

Ham and Cheese Cornbread

Preparation time:
  25 minutes
Total cooking time:
  30 minutes
Makes 16 pieces

1 cup self-raising flour
1 cup cornmeal
1 cup grated cheddar cheese
3 thin slices (100 g) ham, chopped
1/3 cup finely chopped parsley
1 cup milk
1/4 cup olive oil
2 eggs

1. Preheat oven to moderate 180°C. Brush a 30 x 20 cm shallow rectangular cake tin with melted butter or oil. Line base and sides with paper; grease paper.
2. Sift flour into bowl. Add cornmeal, cheese, ham and parsley. Make a well in centre.

Ham and Cheese Cornbread.

3. Add combined milk, olive oil and eggs to dry ingredients. Stir with wooden spoon until just combined; do not overbeat.
4. Pour mixture into prepared tin; smooth surface. Bake 30 minutes or until skewer comes out clean when inserted into centre of cornbread. Stand bread in tin for 3 minutes before turning out onto a wire rack to cool.

Note: Yellow cornmeal can be found in most supermarkets and health food stores. It is also known as polenta. Cornbread is best eaten on the day it is baked.

Choux Puffs with Savoury Fillings

Preparation time:
  1 hour 15 minutes
Total cooking time:
  30 minutes
Makes 16 puffs

60 g butter
³/4 cup water
³/4 cup plain flour
3 eggs, beaten

Salmon Filling
60 g butter
¹/4 cup plain flour
1¹/4 cups milk
125 g can red salmon,
  drained, skin and
  bones removed
2 teaspoons lemon juice
1 tablespoon
  mayonnaise
¹/3 cup finely chopped
  chives

Cheese Filling
20 g butter
125 g button
  mushrooms, thinly
  sliced
60 g butter
¹/4 cup plain flour
1 teaspoon freshly
  ground black pepper
1 cup milk
¹/4 cup cream
¹/2 cup grated cheddar
  cheese
¹/4 cup finely chopped
  parsley

1. Preheat oven to
moderately hot 210°C
(gas 190°C). Brush a
32 x 28 cm oven tray
with melted butter.
Combine butter and
water in medium pan.
Stir over low heat until
butter has melted; bring
to boil.
2. Remove pan from
heat, add flour all at
once. Beat until smooth
using a wooden spoon.
Return to stove, heat
until mixture thickens
and comes away from
side of pan. Remove
from heat, cool slightly.
Transfer mixture to
large mixer bowl.
Add eggs gradually,
beating until mixture is

glossy and thick.
3. Spoon heaped
tablespoons of pastry
onto prepared trays.
Sprinkle with cold
water. Bake 15 minutes.
Reduce heat to
moderate 180°C, bake
further 15 minutes or
until crisp and browned.
4. Cut puffs in half,
remove any uncooked
mixture. Return puffs
to oven for 3–4 minutes
or until dry. Spoon
filling into base of each
puff, replace tops and
serve immediately.
5. *To make Salmon
Filling:* Heat butter in
medium pan; add flour.
Stir over low heat
2 minutes or until flour
mixture is lightly
golden. Add milk
gradually to pan,
stirring until mixture is
smooth. Stir
continuously until
mixture boils and
thickens; boil further
1 minute; remove from
heat. Stir in flaked
salmon, lemon juice,

*Stir flour mixture until it thickens and
comes away from sides of pan.*

*Sprinkle heaped tablespoons of pastry
with cold water.*

Choux Puffs with Savoury Fillings.

mayonnaise and chives; stir gently to combine.

6. *To make Cheese Filling:* Heat butter in medium pan, add mushrooms. Cook over low heat for 3 minutes or until mushrooms are just tender; add flour and pepper. Stir over low heat for 2 minutes or until flour mixture is lightly golden. Add combined milk and cream gradually to pan, stirring until the mixture is smooth. Stir continuously until the mixture boils and thickens; boil for a further 1 minute; remove from heat. Stir in cheese and parsley.

Cut puffs in half and remove any uncooked mixture from centre.

For Salmon Filling, stir salmon, juice, mayonnaise and chives into flour mixture.

Individual Pumpkin Quiches

Preparation time:
25 minutes + 15
minutes refrigeration
Total cooking time:
45 minutes
Makes six 12 cm quiches

1 1/2 cups plain flour
90 g butter
2–3 tablespoons iced
water

Filling
2 teaspoons oil
2 rashers bacon, finely
chopped
1 leek, sliced
3 eggs, lightly beaten
1/2 cup cream
3/4 cup cooked, mashed
pumpkin (250 g raw)
3/4 cup grated cheddar
cheese

1. Preheat oven to
moderately hot 210°C
(gas 190°C). Sift flour
into a large mixing
bowl; add chopped
butter. Using fingertips,
rub butter into flour for
2 minutes or until
mixture is fine and
crumbly. Add water,
mix to a soft dough.
Turn onto lightly
floured surface, knead
1 minute or until
smooth. Store, covered
in plastic wrap, in
refrigerator for
15 minutes.
2. Roll pastry between
two sheets of plastic
wrap, large enough to
cover six 12 cm flan
tins. Cut a sheet of
greaseproof paper large
enough to cover pastry-
lined tin. Spread a layer
of dried beans or rice
evenly over paper. Bake
for 10 minutes. Remove
from oven; discard
paper and beans.
Return pastry to oven
for 5 minutes or until
lightly golden.
3. *To make Filling:*
Combine oil, bacon and
leek in a medium pan,
stir over medium heat
for 5 minutes or until
lightly browned, cool.
4. Combine eggs and
cream in a large mixing
bowl, whisk until just
combined. Add
pumpkin, bacon
mixture and cheese,
stir until combined.
5. Pour filling into
pastry shells. Reduce
the heat to moderate
180°C. Bake for
25 minutes or until
filling is lightly golden
and just set.

Note: Quiches can be
served warm or at room
temperature. Cut in half
for finger food or leave
whole for lunch.

Asparagus Frittata Fingers

Preparation time:
20 minutes
Total cooking time:
30 minutes
Makes about 20 fingers

1/2 cup self-raising flour
6 eggs, lightly beaten
1/2 cup oil
2 medium (200 g)
zucchini, grated
3 spring onions, finely
chopped
1 1/2 cups grated
cheddar cheese
340 g can asparagus
spears, drained

1. Preheat oven to
moderate 180°C. Brush
two 26 x 8 x 4.5 cm
bar tins with oil, line
base and sides with
paper; grease paper. Sift
flour into bowl, make a
well in the centre. Add
eggs and oil, whisk
until just combined.
2. Add zucchini, spring
onions and cheese, stir
until combined.
3. Spoon mixture
evenly into tins. Lay
asparagus spears
diagonally over mixture.
Bake 30 minutes or until
lightly golden. Turn out
of tins, remove paper,
cut into diagonal
fingers. Serve warm or
at room temperature.

Individual Pumpkin Quiches (top)
and Asparagus Frittata Fingers.

Chilli, Garlic and Parmesan Crescents

Preparation time:
10 minutes + 30
minutes refrigeration
Total cooking time:
20 minutes
Makes 80

1¹/3 *cups plain flour*
100 g *grated parmesan
cheese* (1¹/4 *cups*)
pinch chilli powder
¹/4 *teaspoon garlic salt*
100 g *butter, chopped*
2 *egg yolks*
*chilli powder, extra
garlic salt, extra*

1. Preheat oven to
moderately hot 210°C
(gas 190°C). Line two
32 x 28 cm oven trays
with baking paper.
2. Place flour, cheese,
chilli, salt and butter in
food processor bowl.
Using the pulse action,
press button for
15 seconds. Add egg
yolks. Press button for
10 seconds or until
mixture forms a dough.
3. Turn onto a lightly
floured surface and
shape into a 20 cm long
log. Cover with plastic
wrap and refrigerate for
30 minutes.
4. Cut the log into
5 mm-thick rounds.

Cut each round in half.
Arrange crescents on
prepared trays 5 mm
apart. Sprinkle lightly
with extra chilli
powder and extra
garlic salt.
5. Bake 20 minutes or
until lightly browned
and crisp. Transfer to
wire rack to cool.

Grand Marnier Pâté

Preparation time:
15 minutes + 6 hours
refrigeration
Total cooking time:
10 minutes
Serves 8

100 g *butter*
500 g *chicken livers*
1 *medium onion,
chopped*
1 *clove garlic, crushed*
¹/3 *cup Grand Marnier*
¹/3 *cup cream*
¹/2 *teaspoon dried sage*
¹/2 *teaspoon dried
thyme*

1. Heat butter in a
large heavy-based pan.
Add livers, onion,
garlic and Grand
Marnier. Stir over a
medium heat until
livers are almost
cooked and onion is
soft. Bring to the boil,
simmer 5 minutes.
Remove from heat and
cool slightly.
2. Place mixture in
food processor bowl.
Using pulse action,
press button for
30 seconds or until
mixture is smooth. Add
cream and herbs,
process for a further
15 seconds.
3. Pour mixture into a
3-cup capacity
ramekin, cover with
plastic wrap and
refrigerate for
6 hours, until firm.
Serve with melba toast
or crackers.

HINT
You can buy melba
toast at supermarkets.
To make your own,
remove the crusts
from slices of fresh
bread. Flatten with a
rolling pin and cut
into desired shapes.
Dry bread in 210°C
(190° gas) oven for
10 minutes.
Alternatively, toast
white sandwich bread
on both sides, remove
crusts and slice
through the centre
with a serrated knife,
so that each slice is
very thin and toasted
on one side only.
Toast the other
side lightly.

*Grand Marnier Pâté (top) and
Chilli, Garlic and Parmesan Crescents.*

Spicy Sausage Pinwheels

Preparation time:
  15 minutes
Total cooking time:
  20 minutes
Makes 25

125 g sausage mince
1 small carrot, finely
  grated
1 spring onion, finely
  chopped
1 clove garlic, crushed
2 teaspoons tomato
  paste
1 teaspoon curry
  powder
1 teaspoon chopped
  fresh rosemary
1 sheet packaged puff
  pastry

1. Preheat oven to
moderately hot 210°C
(gas 190°C). Line two
32 x 28 cm oven trays
with baking paper.
Combine sausage
mince in a medium
bowl with carrot,
spring onion, garlic,
tomato paste, curry
and rosemary.
2. Spread mixture
evenly over pastry
sheet and roll up to
form a log. Using a
sharp knife, cut log
into 1 cm slices.
3 Lay slices about
4 cm apart on prepared
trays. Bake for
20 minutes or until
lightly golden.

Note: Pinwheels are best
eaten the day they are
made, but can be kept
in the refrigerator in an
airtight container for up
to two days. Reheat in a
moderate oven for
about 15 minutes before
serving. Pinwheels can
be frozen, cooked or
uncooked, for three
months. Freeze them on
oven trays before
transferring them to a
freezer bag, to ensure
the pinwheels stay
separated. Pinwheels
are delicious served with
tomato sauce for
dipping.

Cheese Filo Slice

Preparation time:
  20 minutes
Total cooking time:
  25 minutes
Makes 20 pieces

250 g ricotta cheese,
  mashed
200 g fetta cheese,
  crumbled
1 cup grated cheddar
  cheese
1 egg, lightly beaten
pepper
1 tablespoon freshly
  chopped parsley
1/3 cup milk
1 tablespoon
  self-raising flour
1/4 cup olive oil
10 sheets filo pastry

1. Preheat oven to
moderately hot 210°C
(gas 190°C). Brush a
30 x 20 cm shallow
rectangular cake tin with
oil. Combine the three
cheeses, egg, pepper,
parsley, milk and flour in
a large mixing bowl.
Using a fork, beat until
ingredients are well
mixed.
2. Place five sheets of
pastry onto work
surface. Keep remaining
sheets covered with a
damp cloth to prevent
sheets drying out. Brush
oil over half a sheet of
filo; fold in half. Place
the folded pastry over
the base of the prepared
tin. Brush top of filo
with oil. Repeat oiling,
folding and layering
process with the five
sheets of filo.
3. Spread cheese
mixture over the filo
base; smooth surface.
Repeat oiling, folding
and layering process
with remaining five
sheets of pastry; trim
edges with a sharp knife
if necessary. Mark the
slice into 20 squares; do
not cut through to the
base of the slice. Brush
top with remaining oil.
4. Bake 25 minutes or
until well browned and
crisp. Remove from
oven; cool in tin. Use a
serrated knife to cut
the slice.

*Cheese Filo Slice (top)
and Spicy Sausage Pinwheels.*

Index

Apple
  Kuchen Slice 42, *43*
  Prune and Almond
    Slice *48*, 49
Apricot Coconut
  Crescents 50, *51*
Asparagus Frittata
  Fingers 58, *59*

Bakewell Slice 38, *39*
Banana and Raisin
  Muffins 29, *29*
Brandy Snap Fans *40*, 41
Buttermilk Scones 20, *21*

Caramel
  Hazelnut Scrolls 6, 7
  Nut Tartlets *44*, 45
Cheese
  and Ham
    Cornbread 54, *55*
  and Pear Danish 46, *47*
  Chilli, Garlic and
    Parmesan
    Crescents 60, 61
  Filo Slice 62, *63*
Chelsea Buns 2, *3*
Cherry
  Date and Walnut
    Roll 18, *19*
  Ripple Teacake 12, *13*
Chilli, Garlic and
  Parmesan
  Crescents 60, 61
Chive and Onion Scones
  with Bacon
  Butter *53*, 54
Chocolate
  Eclairs 38, *39*
  Gateau *3*, 4
  Raspberry Swiss
    Roll 14, *15*
Choux Puffs with Savoury
  Fillings 56, *57*
Cinnamon Fritters
  46, 47

*Page numbers in italics
refer to pictures*

Coconut
  Almond
    Macaroons *44*, 45
  Apricot
    Crescents 50, *51*
Coffee Meringue
  Kisses 36, 37
Cranberry Muffins 6, 7
Cream Horns 30, *31*
Crumpets 20, *21*
Custard Tarts *34*, 35

Danish
  Cheese and Pear 46, *47*
  Mini Fruit 34, *34*
Devonshire Splits (Cream
  Buns) 10, *11*

English Muffins 8, 9

Fruit Tartlets 27, *28*

Ham and Cheese
  Cornbread 54, *55*
Hazelnut and Coffee
  Cream Gateau *16*, 17
Honey Nut Strudel 50, *51*

Lamingtons 27, *28*
Lemon
  and Pecan Syrup
    Loaf 18, *19*
  Banana Cake 22, *23*
  Pikelets, Mini 12, *13*

Madeleines 42, *43*
Mini Fruit Danish 34, *34*
Mini Lemon
  Pikelets 12, *13*

Muffins
  Banana and
    Raisin 29, *29*
  Cranberry 6, 7
  English 8, 9

Neenish Tarts 36, 37
Nut and Meringue
  Fingers *48*, 49

Orange
  Bun 22, *23*
  Fig Cake *16*, 17

Passionfruit
  Palmiers *32*, 33
Pâté, Grand
  Marnier 60, 61
Pithiviers 26, 27
Prune, Apple and Almond
  Slice *48*, 49

Quiches, Individual
  Pumpkin 58, *59*

Sacher Slice 24, *25*
Sandwiches 52, *53*
Sausage Pinwheels, Spicy
  62, *63*
Scones
  Buttermilk 20, *21*
  Chive and Onion, with
    Bacon Butter *53*, 54
Shortbread 36, 37
Sour Cream Pound Cake
  10, *11*
Sponge, Easy, with Jam
  and Cream 20, *21*

Teacake
  Cherry Ripple 12, *13*
  Streusel *5*, 5
Treacle and Malt
  Loaf 24, *25*

Vienna Swirls 30, *31*